THE ROSEBUD

GROWING IN THE LIGHT

*A Testament of Becoming Divinely Rooted and
Inspired by Love, Faith, and Wisdom*

NEAL SCOTT

The Rosebud: Growing in the Light

Published by MindWorx Total Wellness, LLC
400 West Peachtree St NW Suite 4, Unit #5222
Atlanta, GA 30308

Cover design: JP Designs Art
www.jpdesignsart.com
Interior design: Natalia Junqueira (Dawn Book Design)
ISBN 978-0-578-628325

Printed in the United States of America

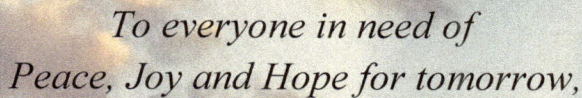

*To everyone in need of
Peace, Joy and Hope for tomorrow,*

I Dedicate my First Book to you.

Each of you are a Reflection of Love & Light.

It is my Prayer that you will begin

Growing in the Light of God and Shining

in a world where His Love will save the Day.

66LIGHT HAS COME INTO THE WORLD. THOSE WHO LIVE BY THE TRUTH AND DO WHAT IS RIGHT COME TO THE LIGHT, SO OTHERS CAN CLEARLY SEE THAT THEY ARE DOING WHAT GOD WANTS.

JOHN 3:19-21

Through God's grace and mercy, we divinely awaken to learn that the seed of the Lord only falls on good soil. In order to receive God's nourishing elements of life, we must be spiritually fed with the truths of the faith and good teaching.

Just as The Rosebud needs air, water, nutrients and light, so does humankind. The only way we as a whole can grow in the fullness of God's light is by receiving substances necessary for proper growth.

The Rosebud has to undergo a series of events at each phase of life with the hope of one day cultivating its athentic beauty. Likewise, God, as our nurturer, planted seeds in us that would cultivate lasting qualities rooted in the soil of his divine love, faith and wisdom.

*"That is why we never give up. Though our outward bodies are dying, our inward spirits are being renewed day by day. For our **light and momentary troubles** are achieving for us an eternal glory that far out-weighs them all."*

2 Corinthians 4:16-17

Contents

We all have stories to tell.
Everyone has their own story,
their own pain. Everyone has
their own moments of happiness,
of suffering, of loneliness, of love,
that have shaped them into who
they are today. Everyone has their
own story, and everyone deserves
someone who is willing to listen to
it. Don't be a dark or sad moment
in a person's story. Be a part of
their light, their happy moments,
and help them through their dark
ones.

Anonymous

Introduction
The Bud of a Rose

he substantive nature of my story gives special importance to the development of identity and awareness in the world. These two dimensions carry far-reaching effects as they both reflect a quality of divine inspiration.

The Rosebud reflects who I am (identity) and the deep knowledge and understanding of my place in the world (awareness). With respect to each element, the spiritual nature of mankind can learn the process that must be followed in order to align with its higher self and to discover the way, the truth, and the life created before the beginning of time.

The Bud of a Rose was birth with the ability to grow in the fullness of light that would in time develop to represent wholeness and meaning. This of course was done in the sight of God after being formed in his likeness to accomplish all he desires, and to achieve the purpose for which he sent it. Therefore, it shall not return empty and always produce the fruit of God's liking.

Even with this glorious discovery, trust is an essential aspect of the process that holds the future of our growth in the palm of his hands. We are wholesomely nourished and held together by joints and ligaments so that we may grow as God causes us to grow while he teaches us to live and walk in the spirit.

As it states in Proverbs 3:5-6,

"Trust in the Lord with all your heart; do not depend on your own understanding. Seek his will in all you do, and he will show you which path to take."

I am the Rosebud, faithfully. This discovery opened my heart to eternal life at the root of existence. There has been a growing realization that the Spirit of the Lord is upon me. My awareness of this revelation increased as life lessons revealed the value of things unseen.

Choosing to trust in God and walk according to his principles and good intentions helped to regulate behaviors and thoughts derived from sinful desires. His word guided my life's course and influenced the evolution of new love, new desires, and a new nature.

Galatians 5:25 declares, "Since we are living by the

Spirit, let us follow the Spirit's leading in every part of our lives." Allowing God to dwell in every aspect of my life unshielded all things that were not like him. The truth is, the Lord does everything in his power to save the brokenhearted whose spirits have been crushed. My spirit was demoralized because I neglected to obey his instructions. Thus, I lost my confidence and hope in him.

God had to break me out of chains, habits and patterns that held me down to the world's standards and ways of doing things. I once read a devotional that ordered me to let Christ reshape and restructure my way of thinking. I was ordered to let his power rebuild me because in him I will find new life. In Christ, I am complete and he will transform me from the inside out.

I was inspired to shift my mindset by focusing on the supernatural influence deeply rooted in the faith of those who trust God. He promised that those who follow him will send their roots into soil near water and will bear fruit (Jeremiah 17:8).

The capacity for growth and continual change had my name written all over it at an early stage in life. However, as the saying goes, there are two sides to every story. In view of all circumstances and conditions, another narrative predominated and devalued my quality of life before I was able to find the right footing. As a result, periods of conflict often evoked emotions and responses unbecoming of my identity and awareness.

A dispirited attitude embracing worldly behaviors, customs, and practices sent me on a wild journey through dark paths and on difficult hikes. The long walk in the wilderness took me down pathways where I found myself wandering around in total darkness. In the wake of trouble and ill will, I became easily affected by lower spirits who tempted me to do wrong.

Despite their impure intentions, my faith and endurance remained strong in the grace of God. I've been on a spiritual journey to access the excellent, virtuous, and true light of my soul. The joy and peace that comes from God brings comfort to my heart and through all I've had to endure, his love never failed.

66 *When troubles of any kind come your way, consider it an opportunity for great joy. For you know that when your faith is tested, your endurance has a chance to grow. So, let it grow, for when your endurance is fully developed, you will be perfect and complete, needing nothing* 99

James 1:2-4 NLT

PHASE ONE

Dawning
OF THE
Light

"The unfolding and teaching of your words gives **light**, so even the simple can understand."

PSALM 119:130

CHAPTER 1
Bud Setting

"In that day, sing about a fruitful vineyard. I, the Lord, will watch over it, watering it carefully. Day and night, I will stand guard so no one can harm it. In the days to come, you will take root. The fields will bud and blossom and fill the whole world with fruit."

(Isaiah 27:2-3, 6)

gapped-tooth, small-town kid, withdrawn and timid, yet inconspicuously full of life's most precious gifts that would later manifest into something of greater value. I recall one glorious day when God spoke to me and said son "the crown of your life begins back at the root of your upbringing." He instructed me to go back to my roots to uncover the untold mysteries hidden deep within my soul.

I was born and raised in the dirty South with no major highways, yet plenty of byways to navigate the plains. My household consisted of both parents and four siblings. The most memorable parts of my early years were established in customs of the church and family traditions.

For a greater insight into my life, I was baptized at a young age and give the ability to walk in purity before God. Thereafter, I joined the music ministry and became a faithful member of the Rosebuds Choir. Much to my excitement, I became overjoyed with showing adoration for God in prayer and song. My mind, heart and body were in harmony with the word of the Lord.

I appeared to live a "normal" childhood. That was the perception considering the propensity for people to conform to the world's standard of normalcy. However, the complex nature of human experiences and emotions often tells a different story. The way we are viewed by the world and the characteristics that define us are shaped by our experiences and emotions. We subconsciously identify with worldly elements and become established in a way that is influenced by human thinking, yet we are not fully aware.

Aristotle once said, "Knowing yourself is the beginning of all wisdom." However, when you're born into a world of sin, wickedness, corruption, and violence, "foolishness is bound up in the heart of a child" (Proverbs 22:15). In the same way, God stated in the very beginning that "every thought or imagination of the human heart was consistently and totally evil all the time" (Genesis 6:5).

The aforementioned are facts proven to be true. So it's not a rude awakening to see people persistently reject acts of righteousness because the truth is not in them.

We do not have a full understanding of who we are at birth, so someone with experience, knowledge, and good judgment should teach us the way of the wise. As noted in Proverbs, there is a saying that requires us to "listen and pay attention to the words of the wise; apply our hearts to God's instructions." This will position us to narrate our lives by way of receiving counsel and advice from a higher source where truth is revealed.

This is why identity is so complex and the word "normal" is easily understood or presents no difficulty. I wouldn't use "normal" to describe the treatment and instructions I received as a child. My life consisted of many different and connected parts throughout childhood that would affect who I was to become. I'm pleased and grateful that a few wise individuals, faithful in all their ways, saw a youngster with a seed inside that had yet to grow in the fullness of God's light.

They followed through on the words planted in their spirit that says to "start children off on the way they should go, and even when they are old, they will not turn from it" (Proverbs 22:6). A timely scripture that rings prophetically in my ears today.

The Lord has been searching for me since child-hood, because he searches all hearts and test the mind to reward each person according to their ways and the fruit of their doing. I was tested, and he knew my anxious thoughts. As Psalms 139:23-24 denotes, God pointed out anything in me that was offensive in any way so that he could lead me along a path of righteousness.

The encounters I had with God's supernatural influence gave me a momentary view and under-standing of who I am, of my place in the world, of the excellence that sets me apart from others, and of a future divinely fulfilled in eternal life.

66 *You made all the delicate, inner parts of my body and knit me together in my mother's womb. Thank you for making me so wonderfully complex! Your workmanship is marvelous—how well I know it. You watched me as I was being formed in utter seclusion, as I was woven together in the dark of the womb. You saw me before I was born. Every day of my life was recorded in your book. Every moment was laid out before a single day had passed* 99

Psalm 139:13-18 NLT

CHAPTER 2

Sing a New Song

"My heart is confident in you, O God; my heart is confident. No wonder I can sing your praises! Wake up, my heart! Wake up, O lyre and harp! I will wake the dawn with my song. I will thank you, Lord, among all the people. I will sing your praises among the nations."

(Psalm 57:7-9)

I learned early on that I was musically inclined and possessed a natural ability for singing God's praises. I wasn't a standout vocalist, but, I could carry a tune. Attending church was regular activity for me. The Bronwood Baptist Rosebuds, as we were affectionately called, led worship every Sunday. We were young but very enthusiastic and cheerful for the opportunity to worship God through music.

I reminisce about the joy I felt every time I stood up to sing. This was the high point of my time in the church. I developed a love for singing and my faith increasingly grew stronger because of it. The Spirit of the Lord was upon me. I wasn't as wise in my own eyes, but I knew there was something extraordinary about the shouting of God's name, O Most High!

"Praise the Lord! Sing to the Lord a new song. Sing his praises in the assembly of the faithful. Rejoice in your Maker. Exult in your king. Praise his name with dancing, accompanied by tambourine and harp. For the Lord delights in his people; he crowns the humble with victory. Let the faithful rejoice that he honors them." **(Psalm 149:1-5)**

I enjoyed making a joyful noise unto the Lord because I felt his peace and comfort. There was something profoundly great and deeply moving about it. I looked forward to being there every Sunday and sometimes on weekdays.

Unbeknownst to me, I was calling out to the Lord with a strong emotion from the bottom of my heart. Oh, what a joyful time it was! I was being used as a musical instrument for God's people in his house where Christ Jesus himself is the cornerstone. As a member of God's family, I felt exceedingly happy and alive.

"We are his house, built on the foundation of the apostles and the prophets. In him the whole building is joined together and rises to become a holy temple in the Lord. Being made part of this dwelling where God lives by his Spirit." **(Ephesians 2:19-22)**

By the end of each song, we had the entire church rocking and lifting holy hands. My intense enthusiasm for praise and worship continued through childhood and increased even more into adulthood. I was conforming to something delightful that seemed removed from the world or everyday life. The light didn't burst forth until many years later that this was all by design. God had made me in this image because he wanted his child to sing along to his melody of love. He marked the sound of music and placed it in my heart.

The ministry of music would eventually manifest my spiritual work and service in the community. It also led to my interest in wanting to learn more about playing a musical instrument. I started with the clarinet and piccolo, which I later decided weren't my speed; I couldn't see myself carrying either one around.

I talked to my dad about buying me a trumpet, and in the sixth grade I became a member of my school's marching band. I admired the features of the trumpet and its capability to produce a great range of sounds. The trumpet, in my opinion, possessed more power than any other instrument. It had a sound that stood out as a symbol of strength long before becoming the shining solid force it is known for today.

During my biblical study, I found that trumpets were blown for many reasons. They were blown during the announcement of good news, over burnt and peace offerings, and to remind God's people that he was with them. People were called by the sound of trumpets to make their way to the mountaintop so they could hear from God. Trumpets were extremely meaningful and significant due to their usefulness in bringing awareness to the presence of God. In the context of this chapter, the following verse attracted my attention because it speaks to my life as a singer and trumpet player joyfully praising God.

"God has ascended with mighty shouts of joy. The Lord has ascended with trumpets blaring. Sing praises to God, sing praises; sing praises to our King, sing praises! For God is the King over all the earth. Praise him with a psalm." **(Psalm 47:5-7)**

I laid my trumpet to rest once I began to venture out and into other things as a teenager. Nonetheless, it's a big part of my story that I believe was divinely inspired by God. After all, he gave me this talent, so why wouldn't he use it for what it was worth? It is also a powerful instrument sounded for praising and worshipping him. God graciously put it in my hands to awaken and to make active a spirit of faith.

66 *My lips will shout for joy*
when I sing praises to you. 99

Psalm 71:23

CHAPTER 3

Family Matters

"For everything there is a season, and a time for every matter under heaven: a time to be born, and a time to die; a time to plant, and a time to uproot."

(Ecclesiastes 3:1-2)

I wouldn't be who I am today without God and family. They have been my rock and strength. I am eternally grateful and blessed to have a loving mother and father, as well as extended relatives who display the true meaning of love. Growing up, I spent a lot of time around family. I had an overprotective mother who, until this day, does not play about her children. Both my parents gave what little they had at all cost, but above everything we shared unconditional love.

As a kid, our family dynamics had a strong impact on my life due to the structure that was set long before I could speak a word. Our bloodline was powerfully built and firmly established so that the family tree would endure the test of time. I credit this to my ancestors who, when I was just a toddler, came together to start a family reunion tradition rooted in love and faith.

Over thirty years later, from generation to generation, we are still building up on our belief that family matters. God certainly blessed us to multiply and fill the earth because he gave life to many aunts, uncles, and cousins. Together in hundreds, we have traveled across the states, broke bread, fought for each other, and shed tears of laughter and sadness for the loved ones we have lost.

We are a strong, godly family with a deep emotional connection. There has been an abundance of joyful and happy moments, especially during the good times. However, as stated in Ecclesiastes at the opening of this chapter, "For everything there is a season and a time for every matter under heaven." It goes on to say, "a time to cry and a time to laugh, a time to mourn and a time to dance."

We have certainly experienced our seasonal droughts and difficult times. There were many days and nights where we have cried and mourned the loss of family members. The pain was unbearable and hard to overcome.

The death of my brother was the most heart wrenching and painful experience ever. Grieving and processing how he was killed took a toll on me. Ricky Bernard Cooper is his name, and he was my oldest sibling. I looked up to him, but he didn't live long enough for me to tell him, or I waited until it was too late.

He lost his life at the young age of twenty-four in a car accident. If the individual he was riding with would have kept control of the vehicle five to seven minutes longer, they perhaps could have made it to my parents' driveway. Sadly, that didn't happen, as the car erratically spun off the road and crashed into an embankment. With so much potential to become the best version of himself, his life was cut short quickly and unexpectedly.

I admired Ricky, and I see several similarities between us today. He was uniquely him and a one-of-a-kind character. Smooth yet different in all his ways. Quiet, but blessed with a glaring light. Unsettled and distressed, though full of determination. He always appeared cool, calm, and collected whenever and wherever you saw him. Ricky was well groomed and fashionable. He also had a fascination with classic cars.

The news of my brother's sudden death sent shock waves across the local area. I recall working with my father over the summer when my aunt frantically drove toward us with the devastating news that Ricky was involved in a serious car accident. The seriousness of his condition was unknown at the moment, but we swiftly rushed to the emergency room.

When we arrived at the hospital, I saw my mother walking back and forth, praying and hoping for Ricky to pull through. We were called into a room, and while entering I noticed a big cross on the wall. The doctor kneeled in front of my mother, and she immediately lost it. When you have a mother like mine who nurtured and gave her all to each of us, it was hard to imagine the grief she would have to endure with the loss of her firstborn child.

As I recall this difficult time of my life, no one knew how much of a heavy heart I carried around. For many days, nights, months, and years after, I cried my eyes out. The outpouring of love we received from family and friends was comforting, yet for me I was affected more than I can explain.

I have an undying love for my family, but I never told Ricky that I loved him because it was just something we didn't express to each other back then. The thought of this, in addition to the overwhelming sorrow, made my heart break.

*"God blesses those who mourn, for they will be comforted."***(Matthew 5:4)**

*"He heals the brokenhearted and binds up their wounds."***(Psalm 147:3)**

The grieving process felt like it would be a lifetime of pain. It went from being acute to complicated, because the feeling was unbelievably true and extremely difficult to manage. I experienced guilt about the thought of living without my brother and accepting the loss. I also agonized about what could have been done differently to save his life.

For a while, I felt they didn't do enough to bring him back to life and they just left him for dead on the table. I never got over those emotions, but after resolving the most intense part of the grief process, I came to accept the reality of the loss.

I miss him every day and still tear up just thinking about his memory. The sadness that I currently feel now may show itself again, but I've learned how to cope. It's been twenty years since he left us, but he will forever be in my heart until the day we meet again in heaven. My first words will be, "You are and have always been my role model. I love you!"

❝ Talk to people about your loss and pain. Don't hide or deny your feelings. Let people know that you need them and ask for help. Consider writing a letter to family and friends outlining your needs. Be patient with those that don't know what to say. Talk about your loved one and share your precious memories. Be grateful for those with the courage to hear your pain and stay with you on this journey. Always remember that you can always talk to God through prayer. ❞

Ellie's Way, www.elliesway.org

PHASE TWO

DARK NIGHT
of the
Soul

" *If you try to hang on to your life, you will lose it. But if you give up your life for my sake, you will save it. And what do you benefit if you gain the whole world but lose your own soul? Is anything worth more than your soul?* "

MATTHEW 16:25-26

CHAPTER 4
Bewildering Grace

"My grace is sufficient for you, for my power is made perfect in weakness."
(2 Corinthians 12:9)

God's grace for humankind is seen and felt by his love, care, protection, and compassion. As the creator of life, he is present and guides the way for all who are willing and obedient. We enable the power and spiritual healing offered through divine grace to reform, cleanse, inspire and strengthen us. When we act in accordance with God's commandments, we receive favor from him. However, anyone acting outside of his instructions will indeed suffer consequences for our disobedience to the word.

Being that I was an inquisitive child who burned with curiosity about everything, I didn't always resist temptation. Although minor, there were instances where I learned my lesson. Case in point, for your amusement and to show my lack of good sense and judgement, the following are a few of those occurrences.

I recall a time when my parents had a disagreement one late night. I overheard yelling, so I wanted to know what the fuss was all about. After jumping out of bed to listen intently, I was caught peeking through the door. My mother loudly uttered, "Take your ass back to bed," so I frantically hurried away. This is a memory I laugh about today. There was an- other time I got lost in the mall after turning around to mind someone else's business. I turned back and couldn't find my parents. Thankfully, a friend of the family recognized me and took me to the security desk so they could page my folks over the intercom.

This next memory should really show you how curious I was. One quiet day, I was lying in bed playing with a sharp object. I had a brilliant idea to use my imagination to create a sword out of a pointy stick. In full superhero mode, I put the sharp edge of the stick down my shorts and it pierced my skin. I cried out for someone to come and relieve me of the pain.

The most jaw dropping of all was when I foolishly thought it would be cool to jump on top of a glass fish aquarium. That didn't go so well because it shattered to pieces with my feet still inside. Several stitches later, the scar on my ankle is a reminder of the intriguing personality I used to have. I share this background information because it lends credence to the fact that I was untamed and all over the place as a kid.

If you're not careful, life can find a way to exploit your doings and vulnerabilities until it becomes an impact on your mental and emotional well-being. The immoral acts of others will take advantage of your exposures and use it to satisfy their own sinful desires. Even when you think you are living by the spirit and out of harm's way, you can get caught up and walk into the wrong place at the wrong time.

I grew up in a town that was uncultivated in many ways. It was nothing for me to cross paths with people, places, and things that were not in alignment with the will of God. Temptation, lust, greed, self-ambition and drunkenness were prevalent in a town of about 500 people at the time. You could find yourself trapped by foolishness and harmful acts set up to ruin and destroy your sense of self. The things you desired most could become stifled by the unpleasant nature of man's way and before you know it, you find yourself lost in world of evil desires.

This may not have been your experience when you were kid, but I'm certain there are too many to name who can attest to my experience. There are even kids at this hour who are living with fear and anxiety as a result of someone else's wrongdoings.

There is an untold number of men and women who have suffered with fear and anxiety since childhood because we are too afraid to speak up about our pain.

I know for me the prolonged distress, heartache, and trauma caused angry outbursts and irritable mood swings. It made me feel disconnected and withdrawn from others. I had no clue that this was all signs of a psychological disorder. My mind had been damaged and I was forced to contend with the disturbing and unsettling effects of emotional stress. I became enraged and confused about my identity and harbored unattended feelings deep inside.

It appeared as if all was well, but I carried a heavy burden that deepened as I bottled up my emotions. I was highly impressionable as a child and therefore susceptible to the oppressive acts of the world. As a person of faith and good morals, keeping straight on the right path was not a thought I took to heart. However, no one ever expects to find themselves in a defenseless position.

It would have suited me well to tread lightly while running the streets but God's way was not in sight. Therefore, I couldn't see clearly where I was going. Consequently, my lack of discipline made a wrong turn. Following closely behind my disobedient acts were wicked and impure hearts looking to unconscionably cause harm.

"Do not be deceived, fooled or misled: "Bad company corrupts good morals, character and habits."

(1 Corinthians 15:33)

Without any defense or protection, I was unseeingly led by immoral acts of kindness that were deliberatly deceiptful and untrustworthy. The unfamiliar sights appeared safe and sound, but trickery lurked beneath the surface. I was indeed fooled by the deceivers of the world. The unconscionable nature of things made it too dark for me to see so I didn't have a clear understanding nor could I rationally decipher how complicated things were about to get. I was lured into a room by "neigborhood floozies" under the influence of an unknown substance. Their minds were foolishly perverted and they behaved in a manner that was wickedly foul.

"Stay alert! Watch out for your great enemy, the devil. He prowls around like a roaring lion, looking for someone to devour. Stand firm against him and be strong in your faith." **(1 Peter5: 8-9)**

There was another kid standing next to me and we both looked utterly confused about what was happening. The women then began to force us close to one another and down on the floor. One of the guilty parties proceeded to motion her hand over my private area and inside my pants. I was unnervingly shaken up and almost lost control of my bladder. They aggressively proceeded to push me on top of the other kid to perform sexual acts. It was all laughs to them as they acted out in a playfully mischievous manner.

I was raised up with Christ, but no one ever told me nor did I read God's Word where it states in Colossians 2:8, "do not let anyone hold you captive through empty and deceptive nonsense that come from human thinking and the elemental spiritual forces of the world, rather than from Christ."

As a young boy who had yet to reach puberty, I was caught up in the bewilderment of life. Severe anxiety didn't set in immediately, because I was still grappling with the perplexity of the matter at such a crucial time in my development. However, in due course, the damaging effects would later dominate my thoughts and actions. Frankly, I didn't know what to make of it, but I began living in fear of what others would think and how they would view me. I was uncomfortable in my own body. The act of engaging in my first sexual experience was gloomy and done in poor taste. Two innocent little boys bewildered by false-hearted examples of moral decency.

If only I would have worshipped without ceasing in my shout to the Lord, the wonders of his mighty love could've comforted and defended me. Thus, I would have "sung of his power; yes, I would have sung aloud of his mercy in the morning; For he would have been my defense and refuge in that day of my trouble. To him, O my Strength, I would have sung praises; For God is my defense, My God of mercy" (Psalm 59:16-17).

If only I would have kept his word habitually before me and set my mind on things above (Colossians 3:2), I could've received his grace and protection when wickedness attacked.

A Meditation on the Excellency of the Word of God
(Psalm 119: 9-16)

How can a young man cleanse his way?
By obeying and living according to your word.
With my whole heart I have sought you;
Oh, let me not wander from your command-
ments!

Your word I have hidden in my heart that I
might not sin against you. Blessed are you, O
Lord!

Teach me your statutes. With my lips I have de-
clared all the judgments of your mouth. I have
rejoiced in the way of your testimonies, as much
as in all riches.

I will meditate on your precepts, and contem-
plate your ways. I will delight myself in your
statutes; I will not forget your word.

66 *My child, don't make light of the Lord's discipline, and don't give up when he corrects you.* 99

Hebrews 12:5

CHAPTER 4

Life in the Wilderness

"Don't you realize that you become the slave of whatever you choose to obey? You can be a slave to sin, which leads to death, or you can choose to obey God, which leads to righteous living."

(Romans 6:16)

can recall several instances where Jesus attempted to wash my feet clean of old ways, but I was too full of myself and consumed with frivolous matters to even notice. **Can you relate?** Oftentimes, we inattentively sidestep God's loving embrace in order to seek pleasure in what the world has to offer as opposed to what he is trying to lovingly do in our lives.

God will make every effort to interfere or interrupt how we persistently move about our day with different signposts, words, delays, or cancellations. However, due to acceptable social norms and expectations to conform, we habitually overlook the truth of his love and sacrifice. In other words, we become defined by groups, our communities and cultural influences, but we fail to see the development of our identity through Christ Jesus. These norms create habits that are not purposefully useful and conducive to our learning and growth, yet we un- consciously make it the underlying basis for how we should behave.

"Do not love this world nor the things it offers you, for when you love the world, you do not have the love of the Father in you. For the world offers only a craving for physical pleasure, a craving for everything we see, and pride in our achievements and possessions."
(1 John 2:15-16)

In my early adult years, I blindly agreed to and accepted what the world had to offer, without realizing the potential effects. I neglected to yield to the signs that God had put in my path to follow. My own heart and inner voice repeatedly condemned my acts of hostility. I engaged in activities that caused war and conflict between the internal and external parts of my existence. Consequently, my actions turned severe and troublesome to a point that I left suffering in silence alone. I had deserted God's plan for my life and I wasn't faithful to his word.

Our relationship suffered because my thinking was not at a level to mentally comprehend the higher calling of God. Thus, I struggled to build a solid foundation where I could stand firm and grounded. Without a foundation in Christ, I became a foolish builder who could not hear the word of God. I was traveling down dark roads which subsequently brought about turmoil. I was fighting with myself to make a good living, but it was all tainted with false hopes.

My pursuit of peace, freedom, and joy were negated by the obsessive interests I had in pursuing undesirable relationships and involving myself with others who had nothing in common. The first obvious manifestation of misplaced priorities was my cry out for help in a world that had no empathy for my disheartened soul. Meanwhile, the mental anguish, emotional pain, and physical distress intensified as I continued to maneuver uncomfortably in a dysfunctional sphere of influence.

As storms began to set in deeper, I became increasingly unstable in nature, with winds blowing painfully and constantly through my ears. The aftereffects and pressure of the raging storms caused my rocky structure to come apart in every way. In Luke 6, Jesus made it clear and plain what will happen when we disobey God's principles and instructions. He stated that, a person who hears the word and does not put them into practice is like a person who built a house on the ground without a foundation. The moment the torrent struck that house, it collapsed, and its destruction was complete.

I made forceful efforts to free myself of the conditions. However, the more I ran and behaved in a manner that did not conform to the standard of God's commands, the deeper I fell into despair. My sinful nature caused a state of disorder to grow in me. As Paul declared in Galatians 6, a man reaps what he sows and will always harvest what he plants. Running through the wilderness was a choice that I made to please the human body. I lacked proper care for the spirit of my soul, because I gave way for chaos to enter.

I went into isolation to avoid people and to keep away from places that didn't serve me well in my current state. With no sense of purpose or direction, I felt frustrated, lost, and discouraged as the walls began to close in and crumble brick by brick. It was frustrating, because I knew the vast potential I carried within to be the best version of myself, yet I was losing it to a world full of foul and loathsome characters, including myself.

The chains around my feet kept me in bondage and pulled me emotionally in different directions. Over time, several traumatic events caused unpleasant emotions and a greater degree of anxiety to erupt. The mental anguish deriving from my associations or interchanges with people brought about adverse consequences. I was threatened, attacked, manipulated, and misused while I desperately moved in hopes of finding peace along the way.

The moves I made would have a continuing effect on my mental and emotional state. I was searching outwardly for freedom in all the wrong places, making it harder to break away from captivity. My physical strength had weakened, and the effects of being imprisoned intensified my mental health condition. During all these severe hardships, I tried earnestly to detach from the stronghold.

Imagine yourself trying to break free from strongholds that have imprisoned your mind to self-imposed stress controlled by the falsehoods of your worldly desires. It was hard for me to move forward in my current condition because I wasn't mentally well enough to fight my own battles. I had to deal with the side effects of undesirable elements inflicting serious harm on my mental, physical, emotional, and spiritual well-being.

It felt like I was sleep walking in darkness while carrying a loaded gun and ready at any moment to pull the trigger. I would've never awakened to see the light of day and my family would've had to put me six feet under. My son would have lost his father and my mother would have to grieve the death of another child. That was practically the choice I was left with at the rate I was traveling.

I was carrying a heavy burden with weight so hard to bear that it caused a dangerously intense mental illness. My ability to function and maintain my business were extremely difficult because I didn't have the mental stability to withstand the overwhelming load of affliction. I had traveled beyond the veil of darkness and deception with the inner depths of a soul that was tired and dying inside. Thus, I was unable to understand and perceive specific aspects of the living world because I walking on the dark side of love.

66 *Those who walk in the darkness cannot see where they are going. Put your trust in the light while there is still time; then you will become children of the light.* **99**

John 12:35-36

CHAPTER 6

The War Within

"So, God abandoned them to do whatever shameful things their hearts desired. As a result, they did vile and degrading things with each other's bodies. They traded the truth of God for a lie. So, they worshiped and served the things God created instead of the Creator himself, who is worthy of eternal praise! Amen."
(Romans 1:24-25)

The years I spent living in fear outside the will of God had a major influence on my mental and emotional state. I was in a constant battle with the higher and lower spirits of my existence. The spiritual nature of the heart, mind, and soul were not existing in a harmonious way. They were misaligned and internally displaced by an external state of living.

The adverse psychological reactions sent me on a foolish and hopeless pursuit of happiness.

The severity of my poor mental health led me to the book of Romans, where the apostle Paul spoke on his battle with doing what is right rather than doing what is wrong. Paul states in his letter to the Romans that he did not understand what he was doing because he wasn't practicing the things that interested him. Instead, he was doing the things that he felt an intense dislike for. His story resonated with me, because I too felt I was behaving in a way that I detested and found intolerable, yet I continued to expose myself to such harmful and undesirable acts.

As with Paul, I wanted to do what was right, but I was in a vulnerable position, and my emotions were all over the place. I found the statement about, "the spirit is willing, but the flesh is weak," to carry an unmistakable truth and a major impact on my life.

"Those who live according to the flesh have their minds set on what the flesh desires; but those who live in accordance with the Spirit think about things that please the Spirit." **(Romans 8:8)**

My mind was afflicted by the spirit of the world. Good sense didn't matter, so it was not uncommon to do mindless things. My thinking was lacking sufficient knowledge and understanding to live at a standard considered to be of the highest quality.

Life changing disruptions in my moral beliefs, behaviors, and practices caused an unfavorable fracture in personal and business dealings.

I lived through a great deal of agony due to my choices in relationships, friendships, and associations. My actions were dictated by the natural desire to think like others who didn't share my values. Thus, I became mentally trapped in a system falsely grounded in reason and disorganized, producing mountains of hostility.

"The sinful nature wants to do evil, which is just the opposite of what the Spirit wants. And the Spirit gives us desires that are the opposite of what the sinful nature desires. These two forces are constantly fighting each other, so you are not free to carry out your good intentions." **(Galatians 5:17)**

My unconscious carelessness turned me loose to perform desperate acts outside the will of God. I didn't realize the seriousness of the tension that I was putting myself through. The wicked schemes of the world and my sinful desires had me in chains. Sex, money, games and deceit were the backdrop of my story. I behaved recklessly and ran with people who put me in danger and at risk of losing everything to this evil world we live in. I was lost, broken, and getting beat by life's obstacles.

I created a sense of comfort in doing things that unconsciously caused destructive interference in the continuation of life. It truly felt as though my soul was being held captive by the elemental forces of the world. As a result, a state of unrest and dissatisfaction were brought on by the crippling effects of my mental, emotional, and financial hardships.

This was my worldview. I was conditioned to identify with the untruths of my identity, which discernibly shaped my self-perception. It was unthinkable to do what God had commanded so that I could live according to his will. Therefore, I took no notice of the messages God was sending me, even though they would save my life.

I ignored his whispers and steadfastly continued to abandon the way of the Lord. His loving attempts to nurture and hold me close in his arms were disregarded as useless. I was openly resistant and being boldly disobedient as I impatiently moved ahead. My discontent with the circumstances intensified because I was failing to yield the right of way required by God's law. The only concern I had was doing what I thought was necessary to fulfill what I wanted out of life. It would have seemed plausible at some point for me to concern myself with what God wanted, but I persistently gave way to my own disoriented direction instead.

Consequently, I continued to spiral downward, became even more disgruntled, feared the unknown, and felt uneasy about life. The struggle to disconnect from the internal and external conflicts was real. I had caused myself so much pain and disharmony in mind and body. The complex patterns of behavior made it feel almost impossible to overcome. My condition was getting worse due to two opposing forces putting an enormous strain on my soul's existence. To my dismay, the conflict kept brewing and remained in effect until it reached a high boiling point. The heat was scorching hot and the ground was dry. Therefore, the fight was on for me to gain control of the situation.

Out of desperation, I often relied on others to satisfy the desires of my heart. I placed my hope of survival in people, despite the ensuing mishaps that could arise. Notwithstanding the fact that I could lose myself in the making, I subconsciously kept moving along a forbidden course in the opposite direction of God's way. The persistence force of the living world had dominated my mental stability for years uncounted. I was unable to manage my emotional well-being, which gave rise to the war I had going on within.

"Clothe yourselves with the Lord Jesus Christ, and do not think about how to gratify the desires of the flesh."
(Romans 13:14)

Through it all, I felt the Spirit of God with me during my darkest hours. I begin praying and asking him to free me of all my fears. I desperately needed him to help me fight off evil spirits that had damaged the health of my life. The shadow of shame that darkened my face misrepresented the truth and showed faulty judgment. I had to seek God's face so he could guide and teach me to fear the Lord and shun evil. He is our ever present help in times of trouble. Therefore, in order to turn away from evil and do good, I had to search for peace in God and work to uphold my trust in him.

I continued to press forward with strong faith and determination. Despite the present conditions, the secret of living was found in the belief that everything can be done through Christ who strengthens me. If it wasn't for my suffering, I wouldn't have had enough power to surrender to God and my cries would not have been heard. The Lord is always close to the brokenhearted and he hears our cry when we call out to him for help.

“ *Since Christ suffered physical pain, you must arm yourselves with the same mind, and be ready to suffer, too. For if you have suffered physically for Christ, you have finished with sin. You won't spend the rest of your lives chasing your own desires, but you will be anxious to do the will of God. You have had enough in the past of the evil things that godless people enjoy—their immorality and lust, their feasting and drunkenness and wild parties, and their terrible worship of idols.* **”**

1 Peter 4:1-3

PHASE THREE

A MESSAGE
FROM *God*

" *Be still and know that I am **God**.* **"**

PSALM 46:10

CHAPTER 7

Be Still

"He calmed the storm to a whisper and stilled the waves. What a blessing was that stillness as he brought them safely into harbor!"
(Psalm 107:29-30)

The way the world is set up, it's inevitable for anyone to fall back into old ways of thinking and acting. We move around constantly with little rest. The burdens of life loads us down. Hardships get heavier and days seem longer. We feel pulled, pushed, pressured to move nonstop around the clock. Like many of you, I was always on the go and couldn't bring myself to relax or rest not even for a second. Having to fight through anxiety attacks made matters worse because it felt like I was losing control and going crazy trying to stay on pace with everything around me.

I was more in tune with being stuck out in traffic with no sense of direction. My mind was never calm and I forced my body to overrule its own exhaustion. It was not until I read the following soft words that I begin to gain some relief from all the congestion, crowding and clogging of the mind.

*"Be still and know that I am God."***(Psalm 46:10)**

Those eight words opened a new dimension of hope. The effects of God's message to me brought about a stillness in nature that was quietly and peacefully serene. I stood in silence as he was guiding me to his resting place safely from distractions so he and I could be alone. A change in movement from complete disorder to an act of physically standing in one place brought about a gentle form of simplicity.

The world around me was silenced as I begin to enter God's place of stillness. Before acquiring a deeper knowledge about the meaning of being still, I defined it from the literal context which says stop moving. It is fact that the word does mean the absence of movement or sound. However, when God stepped in he explained that world's definition is not of his mouth.

When he says to "be still", it carries a much powerful implication. His declaration can cast down strongholds and make the wrath of the storm and the terrors of the earthquake all give way before his mighty right hand. Therefore we must not be mistaken by what it means when God implores us to be still and know that he is who he says he is because nothing is as strong as his word.

God will silence the storms in our life so that we may let go and let him cultivate the habit of stillness in our lives. After realizing what he was intending to do, I stepped back and said God, do you! He wanted me to rest and allow him to move on my behalf. I had no business being on the battle field trying to fight without the armor of God. Once I decided to be still, God said I got you son now go sit down somewhere.

The inactivity caused me to disconnect from worldly passions. I was engaging in less, yet I felt I had more time to focus on things that have eternal value. God knew it was necessary for me to find a quiet space void of distractions. He also instructed me to come prepared with a notebook and pen so that he could write personal notes to me in silence.

I was present for the first time in a while, and a calming spirit filled the room. The atmosphere was free of tension, anxiety, disturbance, conflict, and hostility. All my natural desires were nonexistent, which helped me to open and accept a higher way of thinking. Essentially, God removed obstacles so he could enact his process of restoration.

The time I spent alone with God enlightened me on the steps and practices that must be persistently follow in order to live and walk by the Spirit. Apostle Paul spoke to this "walk" of faith in Galatians: "But I say, walk by the Spirit, and you will not gratify the desires of the flesh", and, "If we live in the

Spirit, let us also walk in the Spirit". I made it an ongoing practice to rest in God's presence. As a result of my continued effort to seek him, I now move different and with a greater purpose. I submit to his will every day that I awaken because I desire to be near him, if only just to listen and hear his voice. "Be still, and know that I am God," played over and over in my mind until it increased to a daily dependence on God.

I understand how intensely hard it is for people to stand still because we always feel the need to be on the move. We also find it hard to do one thing at a time. When God interrupt your movement, stop and listen because he wants to give you so he can take care of your needs.

"In stillness the muddied water returns to clarity."
(Laozi)

When I decided to make stillness a big part of life, I knew God would always be present, especially in times of trouble. Thus, I found refuge, strength, and help in the Lord. The newfound life of being still has helped me to quiet the mental stress so I can connect to God through meditation. This supernatural practice has opened my senses to gather information from my higher source. Stillness has awakened me to the love felt all around and brought me to a state of awareness where the omnipresent desires of God's heart have aligned with my heart's desires.

66 *In the stillness of the quiet, if*
we listen, we can hear the whisper of
the heart giving strength to weakness,
courage to fear, hope to despair. 99

Howard Thurman

PHASE FOUR

ENLIGHTENMENT:
Heart AND *Mind*

" *And the peace of God, which surpasses all understanding, will guard your hearts and your minds in Christ Jesus.* "

PHILIPPIANS 4:7

CHAPTER 8

Desires of the Heart and Mind

"Serve him with a whole heart and with a willing mind, for the Lord searches all hearts and understands every plan and thought. If you seek him, he will be found by you."

(1 Chronicles 28:9)

In the book of Acts, Paul had to weather many storms and was bitten by a snake, but he remained unharmed because of his thinking and hope in God's promise. His thoughts were set on being faithful and acting wise in the face of misadventure. After reaching shore, everyone aboard got to witness the power of God's hand at work during a crisis or disastrous event. Ultimately, Paul's covering kept others safe, because God used and protected him in

85

battle against the storms of life and people calling for his prosecution.

My hardships doesn't compare to what Paul had to endure. Nonetheless, Paul proved that my hope in God alone is enough because he made it through tougher times and never wavered in his faith that he would be saved. His mental inclination or disposition was shaped by the supernatural tendency to lift his mind to higher things. He had established a spiritual mindset that outweighed his light affliction. Paul knew it was only temporary so he kept his mind above the things that were happening around him. That way it wouldn't affect his thinking, feeling, and doing. This is mainly the reason why he was able to commit himself to God's promise and engineer a better course of action during the storm.

It was affirmed that I too can think on spiritual things. This was the only way for me to understand God's plan and to make sense of it all while sailing through my own storm season. I had to follow Paul's lead by putting the mind of God into action and focusing my thoughts on the truth of his Word. God will give us the ability to lift my mind to higher things so that we can overcome our natural, fleshly way of thinking. God will deliver us from the body of death and penalty and will protect, rescue, and save us during times of hardship. God will give us the strength to encourage and uplift others during their own shipwreck or battle with difficulties just as he gave Paul.

"God will put his laws in our heart and write them in my mind." **(Hebrews 10:16)**

He looks deep within the mind and heart to save those who are true and right. I begin serving his law in my mind. By allowing the mind of God to come into my life, the things that I would naturally do gradually begin to grow faint and disappear. My thoughts are within earshot of God with all my heart and with complete trust. Therefore, whenever a storm develops strong winds, the laws in my heart peacefully order me to stop moving completely.

I have been absorbed in thought to accept the will of God's way, which is higher and very different from my natural ways. When God's way of thinking enters, I am able to devote my time and attention to eternal truths and values.

"The mind governed by the flesh is death, but the mind governed by the Spirit is life and peace."
(Romans 8:6)

A shift in narrative was pivotal for me to overcome my fleshly desires. I had to put the mind of God into action in order to gain control of sinful pleasures. The process would be necessary for the building of a firm foundation with learning outcomes that are significant and essential for achieving a higher way of thinking. The process would help me interpret spiritual truths within the guiding light of a more excellent and acceptable course of movement.

I made the decision to put aside the deeds of darkness and put on the shining armor of light and right living (Romans 13:12), the following scripture came to mind as I began to walk in love with Christ:

"Don't worry about the wicked or

envy those who do wrong.

For like grass, they soon fade away.

Like spring flowers, they soon wither.

Trust in the Lord and do good.

Then you will live safely

in the land and prosper.

Take delight in the Lord, and

he will give you your heart's desires.

Commit everything you do to the Lord.

Trust him and he will help you.

He will make your innocence

radiate like the dawn,

and the justice of your cause

will shine like the noonday sun."

(Psalm 37:1-6)

As the Spirit of Christ visibly took shape in my mind, I began to shift higher in every aspect of living. Spiritual aspects of my health and well-being developed and expanded overtime. I learned that a series of actions had to be taken in order to build up the human soul or lower self. The unredeemed aspect of my character was made aware, step by step, of its spiritual soul or higher self that exists on a greater dimension and in opposition to the narrative set forth by the world's influence.

Conformity of the human soul (lower self) versus nonconformity of the spiritual soul (higher self) were recognizably different in nature from one another. Although I had experienced a significant shift, I was still living in a world marked by wrong-doings. It took a lot of discipline and hard work to prevail over the circumstances. I needed God to teach me the way of the wise to gain better insight and understanding of an obedient heart. Following God's teachings impacted my life because they helped to influence sound judgment and I was enlightened with the open mind of Christ living in me.

I relate this time of my life back to Paul's journey after he found himself faced with doing what the Spirit of God was directing him to do. He had a high-ranking assignment that called for him to not only listen but to also make tough decisions on the ground. The choice between good and evil would have a profound effect on the success, survival, and well-being of others. He followed the commands of

God because he didn't want to lean on his own understanding and the way out required wise guidance.

The chances of surviving a catastrophe were uncertain. If he had acted on what man was instructing him to do, the fear of death would have taken over. He also would have been compelled to make irrational decisions. Thankfully, Paul listened, obeyed, and calmly rested in God's presence while being guided to safety.

As with Paul, Listening and obeying carried me to victory. Letting go of my way, so I can let the wisdom from above enter, purified my heart and removed obstacles to achieving a higher way of thinking. I died to my old thoughts, strategies, and actions and concerned myself instead with the conscious spiritual awakening, needs, and wishes of God. It was no longer a do or die mission, but a **DIE TO DO MISSION!**

I steadily began to accomplish what I was called to do by following the instructions that are all-important and of high priority to fulfilling the mission. I actively kept the process of restoration alive by making every effort to become spiritually discerned.

"The person without the Spirit does not accept the things that come from the Spirit of God but considers them foolishness and cannot under- stand them because they are discerned only through the Spirit."

(1 Corinthians 2:14)

A light source moved within my soul to clear a space, allowing access to the element of consciousness and thought. Elemental forces of the world such as uncleanness, hatred, anger, and selfish ambition were changed into spiritual energies that affected the qualities of eternal nature that are unseen. The effects brought into being a new life that exists at the turning point of identifying with the spiritual soul. A seed of love was planted in my heart where the nurturing of stillness and peace settled in the spirit.

A newly structured foundation was set that opened the way to the path of transformation. The strength, endurance, and passion required for sustaining mental and physical activity were rooted in the seeds of faith and wisdom. My mind was lifted to higher things, and that which once held me captive to the law of sin no longer had control over my body.

Thanks be to God for his goodness to me. I can now make sense of the world because I understand God's plan for my life through the ability to think on spiritual things from the heart.

66 *Do not conform to the pattern of this world but be transformed by the renewing of your mind. Then you will be able to discern what is the good, pleasing and perfect will of God.* **99**

Romans 12:2

CHAPTER 9

Spiritual Disciplines & Practices

"Guard your heart above all else, for it determines the course of your life." **(Proverbs 4:23)**

The truth was made known that God is the authentic source that places a covenant around my heart and soul to be fully restored. This was an agreement between God and myself. He made promises and I accepted his commands to abide in him. The spirit would become free to learn the ways of Jesus Christ, so that I may walk in the way of goodness and keep to the paths of righteousness. God is the shield for those who walk uprightly and he guards the paths of justice. (Proverbs 2)

I was instructed to apply my heart to receiving and understanding God's word. Wisdom will then enter my heart and knowledge would be pleasant to my soul. The Holy Spirit advised me to completely commit myself to the Lord so that his words would become fixed in our hearts. As God examined my heart and mind, I was setting out to begin serving him with all of my soul.

In order for my soul to awaken its spiritual nature, I had to focus my mind on the desires of God's heart. The only way I could inherit his best is by getting to know him more closely. This would allow me to see God for who He is really is and begin to understand what he wants to accomplish in me. I wanted to connect with his passion, mission and purpose in the world.

A rise in my spiritual connection with Christ influenced my doings, which ignited underlying values and motivations within the soul. Through my bodily condition, I summed up in myself the elements that are imperative to establishing wholeness and meaning in the physical world. I visited the website Pursuing Intimacy with God and came across an article titled "The Desires of God's Heart. The author made the following key point that I think we all should pay close attention to.

> **"God wants to touch and change our hearts so that we will have the same heart and the same desires and interests and priorities that He has. If He does not do this, we will never be "people after God's own heart", and we can never be one with God and have close fellowship & intimacy with Him. We need to be one with God and in complete unity with Him, in order to have intimacy with Him."**

Accordingly, I began a course of action that would position me to achieve the same heart, desires, interests and priorities as God. I made it obligatory that I cut time out of my day to focus more on producing these delightful outcomes.

The principles and practices of God's teachings would help in creating new habits that would align with the way of the Lord. I knew my prayer life wasn't the best, so the first act of fellowship and intimacy I needed to build up on was my prayer life. This was a spiritual discipline that required constant practice because I never made praying and calling out to God a priority. I had to submit myself to him morning, noon and night, so that all things of this world would cease to exist in time. Prayer revealed the heart and mind of God. The gift of prayer is an activity expected of and given to all followers of Christ.

"Be joyful in hope, patient in affliction, faithful in prayer." **(Romans 12:12)**

The act of doing and practicing things from the spirit would help me to become more like Jesus. Therefore, I began reading scripture, meditating on the word, worshipping in spirit and truth, serving with other believers, and learning about God's love and grace. These were my daily activities.

- Praying
- Reading
- Worshipping
- Serving
- Learning

I was motivated to do each of them as much as possible because I wanted to be and live rightly like Jesus.

1 Timothy 4:7-8 says: *"Train yourself to be godly. Physical training is of some value, but godliness has value for all things, promising benefits for both the present life and the life to come."*

The purpose is for us to discipline ourselves to do godly things in a practical way. It was inspiring to know that everything I was doing had been taught and modeled in the Bible. Therefore, each spiritual discipline was divinely purposed. My mind, soul, and body felt refreshed after having completed one of the above activities. I regained strength and energy to keep going, doing, and living right for God. My spiritual health improved and had a strong effect on my overall well-being.

Several scriptures throughout my study are profoundly mentioned in this book. They have all contributed to my growth in some way, shape or form. Had I not taken the time to focus on producing better results, I would not have acquired the same heart, desires, interests and priorities as God.

Each spiritual discipline demonstrated the truth and proved to be a means for having the right kind of heart. I strongly believe that all was breathed out by God for the purpose of training his people in righteousness and to prepare us for the good work that is to follow. The deep understanding derived from rightly practicing good Christlike behavior, positioned me to become "one with God and on the same page as God."

66 *If anyone speaks, they should do so as one who speaks the very words of God. If anyone serves, they should do so with the strength God provides, so that in all things God may be praised through Jesus Christ. To him be the glory and power for ever and ever.* **99**

1 Peter 4:11

CHAPTER 10

The Beginning of Wisdom

"My child, pay attention to what I say. Listen carefully to my words. Don't lose sight of them. Let them penetrate deep into your heart, for they bring life to those who find them, and healing to their whole body." **(Proverbs 4:20-22)**

W ise advice from a father! There is nothing like godly wisdom. If you are stressed out about life and need good guidance to make it through the day, get you some godly wisdom. If you are tired of making poor choices and need to be taught a lesson on good judgment, get you some godly wisdom. If you are lost and need to find your way back home, get you some godly wisdom. If you are sick and tired of being sick and tired, get you some godly wisdom.

There is no way around it, we all need the wisdom of God in our lives. The beginning of wisdom starts with listening, paying attention, learning and taking his words to heart.

"My child, listen to me and do as I say, and you will have a long, good life. I will teach you wisdom's ways and lead you in straight paths. When you walk you want be held back, when you run you won't stumble. Take hold of my instructions; don't let them go. Guard them, for they are the keys to life."
(Proverbs 4: 10-13)

I'm certain God dropped the mic after that verse. He meant what he said and can back it up with countless stories and testimonies of his amazing power. His saving grace is no secret because we all have free and unlimited access into the blessings of God. "For he does not show favoritism." Romans 2:11. We just have to be willing to study, meditate and apply the truth of his power in any and all circumstances we face.

In the book of Proverbs, Solomon wants to teach people wisdom and discipline to help us understand the insights of the wise. The wisdom coming out the world is not the same as the wisdom received from God because fear of the Lord is the foundation of true knowledge.

"Do not be wise in your own eyes; fear the Lord and shun evil. This will bring health to your body and nourishment to your bones." **(Proverbs 3:7-8)**

A Meditation on the Excellency of the Word of God
(Psalm 119: 105-112)

Your word is a lamp to guide my feet and a light for my path. I have sworn and confirmed that I will obey your righteous judgments.

I have suffered much, O Lord; restore my life again as you promised. Accept my offering of praise and teach me your regulations.

My life constantly hangs in the balance, but I will not stop obeying your instructions. The wicked have set their traps for me, but I will not turn from your commandments.

Your testimonies are my treasure; they are my heart's delight. I am determined to keep your decrees to the very end.

PHASE FIVE

NEW NATURE.
New Self.

" *Put on your new nature and new self which was created according to God, in true righteousness and holiness.* **"**

EPHESIANS 4:24

Form a mental image of yourself walking in the spirit of peace.

Your view is amazing and you can clearly see God's most beautiful creations. The harmonies of life are seen and felt. There is a soothing fusion of elements flowing within your spiritual being.

While looking ahead on your path, you discover the true essence of God's greatest gifts to humankind. Your awareness of his work as the architect of all things made reveals how powerful the mighty hand of God can be.

"He holds in his hands the depths of the earth and the mightiest mountains peaks. The sea belongs to him, for he made it. His hands formed the dry land, too"

(Psalm 95:4-5)

You begin to imagine your own gifts and God's role in creating you in his image to become who you are destined to be. You acknowledge in your heart and mind that because of God, you are and will be who he destined you to become. You are instructed on everything you must do and every move you must make to stay on the right path toward your divine destiny. God has your clear and undivided attention. Your mind is renewed. You heart is purified. Your soul is restored. Your body is healed. Your spirit is cleansed.

Your roots are anchored.

You stand on moral grounds.

Your foundation is strong and stable.

You represent wholeness and meaning.

You are free and full of joy. Life is simple.

You have awakened to the desires of God's heart.

Now imagine the world and the state of things as they exist today. Is it a life worth living, or do you see yourself aligning more with God's way, the one who created you in his likeness?

The only thing standing between you and your journey's end are the choices you make.

"Whether you turn to the right or to the left, your ears will hear a voice behind you, saying, 'This is the way; walk in it.'" **(Isaiah 30:21)**

66 *When you walk, you won't be held back; when you run, you won't stumble. Take hold of my instructions; don't let them go. Guard them, for they are the key to life.* **99**

Proverbs 12:13

CHAPTER 11

Wise Creation

"For all creation is waiting eagerly for that future day when God will reveal who his children really are."
(Romans 8:19)

An unopened seed of a rose. Planted and produced by the warmth of God's love. Made into existence and given life above the earth's surface. Seeded to bring more meaning and potential to the upper layer of earth through its enlightened expression of God's heart, desires, interests and priorities. Created out of nothing, but purposed for greatness. The Rosebud, I AM! Fearfully and wonderfully formed in the great light and image of God.

"And God said, "See, I have given you every herb that yields seed which is on the face of all the earth, and every tree whose fruit yields seed; to you it shall be food."
(Genesis 1:29)

God made sure everything he created in the beginning was good to ensure the foundation was set for the plans he had in mind to give his creation a future and a hope. God was already planning ahead before he gave us the breath of life and the knowledge of truth. He declared that he planned to prosper and not harm us so that when we call on him and pray, he will listen. God made it clear from jumpstart that if we seek him with all of our heart, we will find him and he will bring us back home to our own land. He said it plainly in Jeremiah 29 verses 11-14.

As it states in Romans 8, the suffering I had to endure is nothing compared to the future glory God has revealed. I've been liberated from bondage and brought into glorious freedom with the children of God. And now it makes perfect sense why I he created me to become a singing Rosebud grounded in faith in my mother's womb.

I became rooted with the hope of building up in God's foundation of love from the moment he said, "Let there be light." Through the mighty power at work within the depths of the soil, the root system of the Rosebud favored growth at its highest potential. In this way, I would become strengthened in the faith that proper care and management from a higher source is essential to being nurtured and anchored in truth.

God revealed to me that the Rosebud represents a combination of qualities, with love being its greatest gift. It has distinctive traits that are known to stimulate the mind and affect human energy. To a great depth, it exemplifies purity and grace, like an imaginative piece of artwork created to give life to the inner works of true power. By the show of its uniqueness and one-of-a-kind features, the Rosebud stands out, showing the capacity to develop as a kindhearted vessel that can be useful in time for every good work.

With a myriad of uses, the Rosebud was sought out and set apart on a mission in a bed of its own. The true essence of its use would amass together believers of a source that is trustworthy and reliable. Lives will be transformed as their faith grows stronger in the truth they are taught about the abiding and living Word of God.

God lovingly directs the heart into a full understanding of how wide, how long, how high, and how deep his love is (Ephesians 3:18). As the roots of the Rosebud grow down into God's love, his strong foundation will take hold and say do not fear, I will help you and I will give patient endurance and encouragement when your faith is tested.

The Rosebud must endure phases of development in the process of being made complete with all the fullness of life and power that comes from God (Ephesians 3:19). During each phase of life, a higher level of consciousness is discovered. The Rosebud is watered with the wisdom needed to produce a greater knowledge and understanding of the power and light seen within.

By the practice of good judgement and know-how, the Rosebud becomes strengthened from its core with the ability to discern and listen for instruction. As stated in Proverbs 18:15, "The heart of the discerning acquires knowledge, for the ears of the wise seek it out." Furthermore, in Proverbs 19:27 it's said, "If you stop listening to instruction, my child, you will turn your back on knowledge."

In order to grow accordingly, the Rosebud must know that wisdom is essential for the prolongation of life and, as such, the Lord preserves every living thing under the sun with knowledge. When instructions are acceptably followed, the Rosebud undergoes a life-changing experience through the connection, in all its fullness, to the main source of light. "For in Christ lives all the fullness of God in creation" (Colossians 2:9).

God makes all creation alive with Christ. "For He holds the whole body together with its joints and ligaments, and it grows as God nourishes it" (Colossians 2:19). The growth of the Rosebud requires many years of mastery in order to develop gradually toward a more fulfilling and purpose-driven life.

Therefore, to be made alive in Christ with the hope of being rooted and built up in him and to be strengthened in the faith as we are taught, the Rosebud must be wise in all its might to withstand the uncultivated grounds. The Rosebud, I AM!

❝ *The wise are mightier than the strong, and those with knowledge grow stronger and stronger.* **❞**

Proverbs 24:5

CHAPTER 12

The Land Is Yours

"The land you will soon take over is a land of hills and valleys with plenty of rain. A land the Lord of God cares for." (Deuteronomy 11:11-12)

In my neck of the woods, fields and farmlands existed in great quantities. Although sparsely populated due to a lack of resources and undeveloped land, deep roots existed across the landscape where miraculous signs and wonders had been performed before humankind was created. It was by the power of signs and wonders that we as a people could still blossom in producing a quality presence through the belief that all things were possible. The state of being without some of life's most precious commodities demonstrated the truth of God's power to sustain his creation one day at a time.

Fields were used for cultivation in the process of preparing the soil for planting crops. As with a field full of cultivated plants such as fruits or vegetables, we humans have in our possession the power to produce fruit of our own. However, the process is heavily conditional on the acceptance of God's nurturing and the following of his way. It was promised from the beginning that anyone who grew up on good soil would be a true representative of its kind. According to Luke 8:15, those characteristics represent honest, good-hearted people who hear God's Word, cling to it, and patiently produce a huge harvest.

Living in the south, good farmlands were like gold mines. When the sower went out to sow his seeds, he did it with care, due to the abundance of resources that would be produced. This source of wealth was preserved by people who were faithful in their mission to nurture growth from the ground up. The process of maintaining their land seemed rather difficult, but the result appeared fruitful. I'm certain it required a lot of time and attention to detail for the farmland to grow quality pasture.

People regarded good farmlands as a valuable resource because of the richness contained in producing something desirable for greater means. There are several elements that contributed to the building of land in the most favorable conditions. The purpose was to grow grassland suitable for pasturage. Therefore, soil quality, cli- mate, and location were all essential means for cultivating grounds.

There is a shared interest between humankind

and grasslands because of the commonalities that exist in the nurturing, feeding, and strengthening of good soil. Humankind and farms alike are both significantly meaningful in that each provides a host of benefits. During my research, I ran across an article on Conservation.org that emphasized the importance of preserving farmlands for economic, environmental, and sociocultural gains. Spiritually speaking, humankind also serves a key part in the natural world. Therefore, we too are worth preserving due to the impact of our activity on each of the conditions. The following excerpt from that article will highlight the phenomena of farms in relation to the connection they have with human nature.

> Farms do not stand alone. Each is an anchor of stability for other nearby farms. Each is a thread in a web of neighboring farms, farm businesses, and other human endeavors that support and rely upon each other. When one thread is lost, the negative consequences ripple through the community. When many threads are lost, there comes a point when the web fails— when farms and farm businesses no longer have the mutual support needed to keep the local farm economy viable.

Let's read the aforementioned statement again but use humankind in place of farms. If you listen, you'll hear several similarities in creation. My declaration to God's people would read:

Having been created in the likeness of God, we're never alone because he stands beside us (Psalm 121:5). God's unfailing love and faithful- ness in our lives keep us rooted so that we may teach and counsel each other with all the wisdom he gives (Colossians 3:16). When one lost soul is unable to find his or her way, the foundation weakens and in time becomes uprooted due to instability. When many souls are lost, the soil quality becomes rocky as a result of the stormy climate and environmentally fragile location.

Why make this comparison between two very distinctive creations? Well, one easy way to put it is that behind everything in creation sits a Creator who had a vision for the created. Therefore, the power of sight gives life to existence through a process called creativity. The creative skill of the Visionary established earth so that he could bring forth grass, seed, and fruit from a tree. Man was formed and a garden was planted in order to maintain life and growth (Genesis 2:8-9). Without God's handiwork, there wouldn't be any farmlands to grow crops or green herbs for food and there wouldn't be any humankind to cultivate or work the land.

" *Listen to me; listen and pay close attention. Does a farmer always plow and never sow? Is he forever cultivating the soil and never planting? Does he finally plant his seeds, each in its proper way, and each in its proper place? The farmer knows just what to do, for God has given him understanding. All of this comes from the Lord Almighty, who is a wonderful teacher. He gives the farmer great wisdom.* **"**

Isaiah 28:26, 29

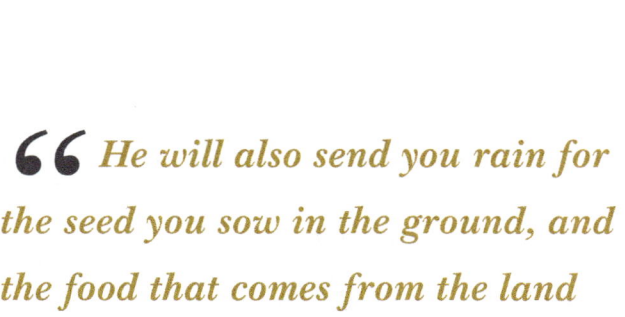

He will also send you rain for the seed you sow in the ground, and the food that comes from the land will be rich and plentiful.

Isaiah 30:23

CHAPTER 13

Sowing Seeds

*"The seed is the word of God. The ones that fell on the good ground are those who, having heard the word with a noble and good heart, keep it and bear fruit with patience." (**Luke 8:15**)*

Good seeds are of great significance and value because they were created to bring forth fruit. Each seed holds a divine place in the heart of God as he makes them grow over time. After the seeds have been planted in our hearts and watered, a growth cycle proceeds before the fruit-bearing process starts. We have to go through a period of development at the root before breaking through the soil. God wants our roots to be planted deep in Christ so that we can grow in him. We find our strength to build up and stand firm in our faith when we follow Christ Jesus.

Seeds carry food and all the instructions necessary for new life. A seed was placed in the ground so that it could grow and be of substance from which humankind would receive nourishment. As such, we were brought into being and given the breath of life on good soil.

Love, faith, and wisdom played a significant role in the nurturing of my soul, and they provided daily bread as I entered God's garden of life. Although the hands of God are unseen, I bore witness to the value of his hard work. The way I remained in him was through the truth of knowing that life on cultivated soil would exist forever if I learned how to produce good fruit.

God spoke life into me by revealing what it will take for my roots to grow down stronger in him. To experience learning, growth, and transformation from a higher calling, accepting and following instructions were required for receiving proper care and management. The Apostle Paul said that if you accept Christ Jesus as your Lord, you must continue to follow him. He further instructed us to let our roots grow down into Jesus so that our lives will be built on him (Colossians 2:6-7).

My wellbeing was impacted by the healing, soothing, and restoring elements of good seeds. I needed nourishment that would renew my mind and change my way of thinking, so the qualities and spirit of Jesus Christ would manifest within my soul. By abiding, listening, and obeying instructions, I gained a greater understanding of how fruit is produced from the Spirit. Learning the process would inspire continued growth and development.

My task was simple. Abiding in God, listening to his commands, obeying his instructions, and producing fruit.

The process was essential for:

1. Building up on God's firmly established and immovable foundation

2. Nurturing roots to grow down stronger into God's redemptive love, faith and wisdom

3. Developing new life by following God's way with all of my mind, heart and soul

4. Walking according to the Spirit of a higher power living in me and guiding me on a path of divine awakening, restoration and transformation.

This helped me to align with my higher source so that I could not only live by the spirit, but also walk by the Spirit of God's light.

A profound statement I meditate on daily:

With man things are impossible, but with God all things are possible. Thus, I should always put my trust and hope in him so he can provide me with the proper care and nourishment for a life well lived. "For hard- ship does not spring from the soil, nor does trouble sprout from the ground." (Job 5:6)

In order to adapt to the harsh environments, deep roots were extremely important for bringing nutrients and water from several feet under the soil. Just as plants and trees depend on their roots for survival in the field, humankind's state of existence in the wilderness rests on having deep roots.

"As long as the earth endures, seedtime and harvest, cold and heat, summer and winter, day and night will never cease." **(Genesis 8:22)**

In the process being nurtured, we rely on the love God has for us because we put our trust in him. "All who live in love live in God, and God lives in them" (1 John 4:16). As we're being rooted and established in love, we are empowered with inner strength through the Spirit of God in our lives, so that Christ may dwell in our hearts through faith (Ephesians 3:16-17). Demonstrate genuine repentance for your misdeeds. Allow God to counsel and share his heart and knowledge with you (Proverbs 1:23). The wise in heart consent to receive orders and instructions (Proverbs 10:8). God will teach you wisdom's ways and lead you along straight paths (Proverbs 4:11).

" The wisdom from above is first of all pure. It is also peace loving, gentle, willing to yield, full of mercy and good fruits. And those who are peacemakers will plant seeds of peace and reap a harvest of righteousness. "

James 3:17-18

CHAPTER 14

Spiritual Nourishment

*"My nourishment comes from doing the will of God,
who sent me, and from finishing his work."*

(John 4:34)

Can you imagine having your own caregiver who regularly provides nourishment necessary for life, health, and growth? How fulfilling would it be to never have to worry about being fed? Sounds satisfying and nourishing, right? In essence, without food, it's simply hard to exist and function day to day. Our physical survival rest on having a tasty meal from time to time. What if our appetite or desire for spiritual food was the same? In order for the substantive nature of our existence to grow in divine favor with God, we need to eat his words.

*"Taste and see that the Lord is good."***(Psalm 34:8)**

Our bodies are created to wholesomely learn, grow, and transform at different stages of life. If we allow God to feed us with his words of faith, we will never have a food shortage, become malnourished or lack energy. God's word provides all the essential nutrients that our body needs. They will help us to continually grow and maintain optimal spiritual health. We can't produce everything we need to function, but the word of God can yield a rich and plentiful harvest.

If we allow the Lord to give us bread, he will take care of us forever and provide all we need to produce fruit of the Spirit. "It is the Spirit who gives life; the flesh profits nothing; the words which I have spoken to you are spirit and are life." He will continue to refresh our souls with good seeds. This is how we are to receive proper nourishment in the process of being developed from God's tree of life.

However, our willingness to be on the receiving end matters greatly. We are purified through our obedience to the truth and through the living and abiding Word of God. In order to build up and grow, we must be sufficiently supported. We are afforded in creation with the opportunity to be spiritually fed by the seeds of God's love, faith, and wisdom.

What if you were to stop moving one day, then gaze out into a grassy field and see standing a tall, beautiful tree of life bearing delicious fruit. A voice whispers and says it's yours if you leave behind your flesh, but you lose it all if you disobey the Word. Your obedience leads to the truth and eternal life. The failure to obey sends you away into the wilderness, while the tree is left to wither and die in a place where the health of your soul lives. Do you go out into the field for spiritual nourishment, or do you stay on a path where there are no substances available to provide the necessary means for life? Choose wisely!

In order to let go and let God take care of us, we must be willing to accept his Word. In hopes of our path being made right, we have to submit to the love, faith, and wisdom of the Highest. These good seeds need sunlight, water, and nutrients to be transported above and down into the root of our existence. Only then, as we begin to follow the process, could we be positioned and prepared to remove the spiritual powers of the world so we can put on our new nature in mind, heart, and soul. **"We will eat all the food we want and live securely in your own land. I will give you peace in the land, and you will be able to sleep with no cause for fear."**

" Abide in me, and I in you. For a branch cannot bear fruit by itself, unless it abides in the vine, neither can you, unless you abide in me. I am the vine; you are the branches. Whoever abides in me and I in him, will produce much fruit. For apart from me you can do nothing. "

John 15:4-5

PHASE SIX

Love IS THE GREATEST _of all_

> " _Three things will last forever,_ **_faith_**, **_hope_** _and_ **_love_**, _and the greatest of these is love._ "

1 CORINTHIANS 13:13

CHAPTER 15

A Gift of Love

"God lives in us, and his love is brought to full expression in us." (1 John 4:12)

ove is essential to the nature of God. It is especially significant in the way he expresses real love to those who share his divine nature. When we reflect the holy and loving character of God, he grants the living soul with the natural gift of love and compassion in his sight for others. As followers of Christ, it is our calling to fulfill God's commandment to love one another. He transformed our hearts to live in him. Therefore, everything must be done in love, because love is from God and he lives in us.

"Love is the greatest! Therefore, it never fails, never gives up, never loses faith. Love bears all things and endures through every circumstance. Love will last forever." (1 Corinthians 13)

We are connected to the divine love in our heart from God. The strength and energy needed for proper growth is found in the root of God's unfailing love. Just like a tiny rosebud that stands in need of water to help transport nutrients within the soil to different parts of the plant, we have to be nurtured in a similar fashion.

I understand why God said to "love each other deeply with all your heart" (1 Peter 1:22).

Love has all the desirable elements, qualities, and characteristics.

Love is the divine nature of becoming one with the Creator of our destiny.

The creator is the source by which we learn the teachings of living a wholesome and meaningful life.

Our souls were made with the thought of love as the greatest and most enduring feature.

We were created to live with pure love in our hearts so that the Creator will have a place to call home.

I bring to your attention a scripture reading from (John 13:7-8) when Jesus washed His disciples' feet and said to them, "You don't understand now what I am doing, but someday you will."

Peter, one of his disciples, protested this activity, but Jesus insisted, replying, "Unless I wash you, you won't belong to me."

Jesus, the Son of Man, was on a mission to glorify his Father by fulfilling a masterful plan in human flesh that would save and redeem all of God's people.

There is no love like the perfect love of Jesus Christ. He makes us all complete. He casts out any feelings of fear, doubt, or anxiety.

The disciples had no understanding of the everlasting grace that would come of Jesus's brotherly affection. It was in his divine calling to love all during his teachings on earth, so just imagine what he must have felt in the final hour as he took great care of his disciples.

Jesus knew that by cleaning their feet he would be setting the example of mindfulness, grace, and self-giving. The divine discipline of his love was intended to help the disciples grow in a relationship with our heavenly Father.

Jesus's course of action was purposeful and significant yet pleasantly surprising to his disciples. Many don't understand the significance of giving and receiving love.

God is love, which made it rewarding for his son to instruct those who follow him to further his lead. He directed them to completely wash each other's feet and the feet of people whom they would inevitably cross paths with on their journeys.

Jesus Christ loved the world so much that He gave everything for it, from His rights and privileges as the unique eternal Son of God, to His very life!

"**For God so Loved the World** that he gave his one and only Son, that whoever believes in him shall not perish but have eternal life. For God did not send his Son into the world to condemn the world, but to save the world through him" (John 3:16-17).

66 *A new commandment I give to you: Love one another. As I have loved you, you should love one another.* **99**

John 13:34

PHASE SEVEN

HOW

Sweet

THE

Sound

" It is only by **God's** grace that
you have been saved! "

EPHESIANS 2:5

ceptable to him. Thus, I was nurtured and provided with resources necessary for continued growth and development. As my roots grew down stronger into the foundation of God's love, a new dimension of light was found.

And so, with the new nature I now possess, it has been revealed by the Holy Spirit that I was chosen for a time such as this to be an instrument for special purposes. God knew that one day I would blossom and reach full development in a manner that would honor him. He knew that I would possess the talent, skills and knowledge to fulfill a mission greater than what the world can deliver and bigger than the eyes can see. God knew that I would carry out his work in the light and inspiration of his unfailing love and faithfulness.

God gifted me with a compelling story so that people will know he's living in me and hearts can be change. My compassion comes from the heart of God and his amazing grace in my life. Who knows where I would be without the sight of wisdom and understanding, sound judgment and discernment. As it states in Proverbs 3: 21-23, they have been life to my soul and grace to my neck. I will go on my way to safety, and my feet will not stumble.

"I was once lost but now found. I was blind but now I see." Thanks be to God! By the power of his love, I will walk the path that was planted for me to grow, in the fullness of time, as one with the light of my salvation.

Thank you for delighting in God's words and reading about my story of redemption! The true essence of God's amazing grace and power have been revealed. Walking in the Spirit and following God's way proved to be more powerful than opposing forces.

This revelation attests to God's ability to do immeasurably more than we ask or think, according to the power that is at work within us (Ephesians 3:20). Through his outpouring of love, manifestation of light, eternal grace, and divine nature, I have clearly seen his invisible qualities (Romans 1:20).

The wholesome teachings of Jesus Christ have anchored my soul in greater knowledge and understanding of how I am to walk in the spirit of God. As I continue to follow his way as the light of the world, I know with all certainty that my life has changed forever.

" *In his kindness God called me to share in his eternal glory by means of Christ Jesus. So, after you have suffered a little while, he will restore, support, and strengthen you, and he will place you on a firm foundation. All power to him forever! Amen.* **"**

1 Peter 5:10-11

PHASE EIGHT

HIGH
Calling
OF
God

Since you have been raised to new life with Christ, set your sights on the realities of heaven, where Christ sits in the place of honor at God's right hand.

COLOSSIANS 3:1

ABOUT THE AUTHOR

NEAL SCOTT is a health and wellness expert who has worked in communities and schools delivering services to men, women, and children in need of physical, mental, emotional, and spiritual guidance. He gives special importance to the concept of achieving optimum health within all dimensions of wellness.

His belief in the notion that good physical health often contributes to good mental health emboldened him to cultivate a practice of total wellness including mental health, physical fitness, emotional nourishment, and spiritual well-being. He indelibly possesses an earnest desire to inspire, uplift, and serve others on their paths to discovering wholeness and meaning.

Scott is a certified counselor with a Master's degree in the field of counseling psychology. He has evolved into becoming a Transformational Coach, as well as an author and speaker.

A servant leader on an important assignment to fulfill God's purpose and will for his life. His mission is to build, grow, and transform lives by inspiring a shift in narratives and coaching people to achieve a higher way of thinking.

His vision is to bring light to paths in a way that guides life decisions, offers a greater sense of direction, and creates meaningful living. He stands on a firm foundation rooted and inspired by the love, faith, and wisdom of God Almighty!

"Because of God's grace to me, I have laid the foundation like an expert builder. Now others are building on it." **(1 Corinthians 3:10)**

I needed God's great strength and power to overcome some of life's most difficult challenges.

Despite the struggle, there was a much deeper revelation of a higher calling leading me beside the still waters.

What I perceived as hardships were the growing pains of being uprooted from God's foundation and living outside his will.

As a result, the good seeds of love, faith, and wisdom could not grow tall and strong without deep roots.

A Meditation on the Excellency of the Word of God

(Psalm 119: 176)

O Lord, listen to my cry; give me the discerning mind you promised. Listen to my prayer; rescue me as you promised.

Let praise flow from my lips, for you have taught me your decrees. Let my tongue sing about your word, for all your commands are right.

Give me a helping hand, for I have chosen to follow your commandments. O Lord, I have longed for your rescue, and your instructions are my delight.

Let me live so I can praise you, and may your regulations help me. I have wandered away like a lost sheep; come and find me, for I have not forgotten your commands.

" Fix your thoughts on what is true, and honorable, and right, and pure, and lovely, and admirable. Think about things that are excellent and worthy of praise. Keep putting into practice all you learned and received from me. Everything you heard from me and saw me doing. Then the God of peace will be with you. "

Philippians 4:8-9

JESUS SPOKE,

❝ I AM THE LIGHT OF THE WORLD. IF YOU **FOLLOW ME**, YOU WON'T HAVE TO WALK IN DARKNESS, BECAUSE YOU WILL HAVE THE LIGHT THAT LEADS TO LIFE. ❞

JOHN 8:12

CPSIA information can be obtained
at www.ICGtesting.com
Printed in the USA
LVHW080236170520
655734LV00003B/12